WITHDRAWN

D1790742

UNIVERSITY SCHOOL LIBRARY
UNIVERSITY OF WYOMING

Cities of the Revolution

WILLIAMSBURG

By Susan and John Lee

Illustrated by Tom Dunnington

CHILDRENS PRESS, CHICAGO

Library of Congress Cataloging in Publication Data

Lee, Susan.
  Williamsburg.

  (Cities of the Revolution)
  SUMMARY: A portrait of a charming colonial capital of Virginia and a history of its activities during the French and Indian and Revolutionary Wars.
  1. Williamsburg, Va.—History—Juvenile literature.
[1. Williamsburg, Va.—History] I. Lee, John, joint author. II. Dunnington, Tom. III. Title.
F234.W7L37   975.5'4252   75-9780
ISBN 0-516-04689-6

Copyright© 1975 by Regensteiner Publishing Enterprises, Inc.
All rights reserved. Published simultaneously in Canada.
Printed in the United States of America.

1 2 3 4 5 6 7 8 9 10 11 12 R 78 77 76 75

CONTENTS

Chapter 1
MIDDLE PLANTATION BECOMES A CAPITAL 5

Chapter 2
BUILDING WILLIAMSBURG 11

Chapter 3
WILLIAMSBURG BECOMES IMPORTANT 19

Chapter 4
PATRICK HENRY LEADS THE WAY 31

Chapter 5
"LIBERTY OR DEATH" 40

Chapter 6
VIRGINIA DECLARES INDEPENDENCE 47

Chapter 7
A FORGOTTEN CITY 53

Chapter 1

MIDDLE PLANTATION BECOMES A CAPITAL

The story of Williamsburg, Virginia, began in London, England, well over 350 years ago. During the rule of King James I, about 100 Englishmen decided to leave England. They were sure they would get rich in America.

The daring men sailed across the Atlantic Ocean in three ships. In sixteen weeks they reached the Virginia coast. It was April of 1607. As the ships neared land, the men saw Chesapeake Bay. While exploring this bay, the settlers found a wide river.

The men sailed 30 miles up the James River and picked a spot for their colony. It was on a peninsula surrounded on three sides by the river. The water ran deep close to shore. Ships could sail up to the bank and tie up to trees on the shore. The settlers named their colony Jamestown, in honor of the king.

Over the years, the area up and down the James River was also settled. Men cleared the forests and built plantations. They grew tobacco and sold their crops to England.

Jamestown was the nearest city for many plantation-owners. They went there to attend court, buy a slave, or enjoy a fair at harvest time. There were few roads, and most people traveled by boat.

Soon, Jamestown became the center of government in Virginia. In 1619, Virginians held their first election in the colony. The planters voted for men to represent them in a legislature. The legislature, called the House of Burgesses, made laws for the Virginia colonists. The representatives, called burgesses, met in Jamestown twice a year to make and pass laws.

As more and more people settled in Virginia, they became unhappy with Jamestown as their capital. The peninsula, always low and marshy, was a breeding ground for bugs that caused sickness. Swamp fever was not the only problem. The strong river tides ate away Jamestown's shoreline. It was hard to keep the docks repaired.

Then, in 1689, England got a new king, William, and his wife Mary. They picked the Reverend James Blair to head the English church in Virginia. Reverend Blair started his job by visiting all the churches in Virginia. He liked a place called Middle Plantation the best.

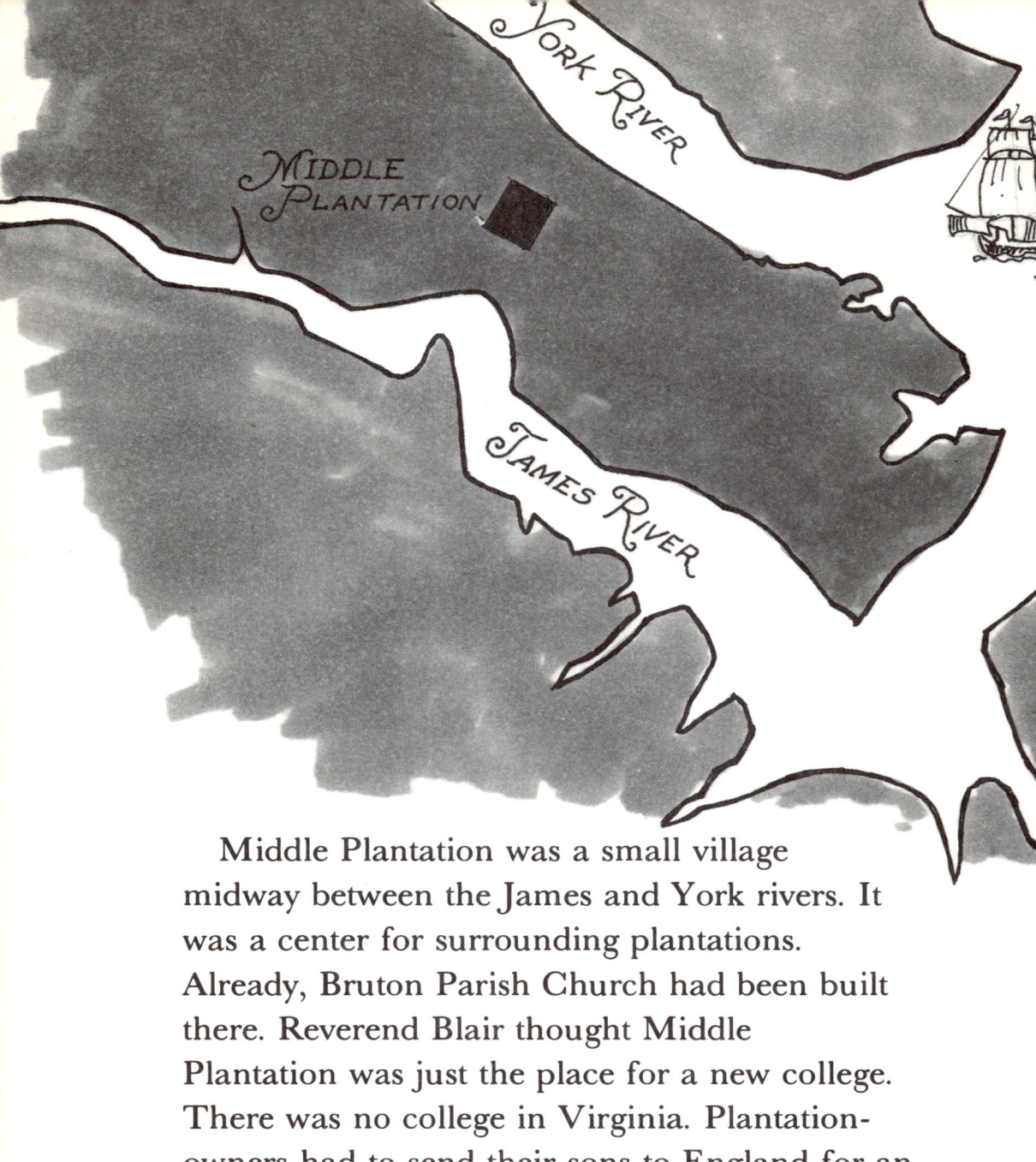

Middle Plantation was a small village midway between the James and York rivers. It was a center for surrounding plantations. Already, Bruton Parish Church had been built there. Reverend Blair thought Middle Plantation was just the place for a new college. There was no college in Virginia. Plantation-owners had to send their sons to England for an education.

The colonists liked Reverend Blair's idea. In 1693 the King and Queen told the young minister to start his school. He began to collect money. Plans were drawn by a famous London architect, Sir Christopher Wren. Two years later, the building began.

The new college was named William and Mary, after the King and Queen of England. It was the second college founded in the New World.

The college was not open long before a fire burned the government buildings of Jamestown to the ground. It seemed like a good time to move the capital to Middle Plantation. Unlike Jamestown, Middle Plantation was on high, dry ground.

The governor of Virginia spoke in favor of moving. In 1699 the burgesses voted to move the capital from Jamestown to Middle Plantation. They also decided to re-name the new capital Williamsburg, in honor of King William.

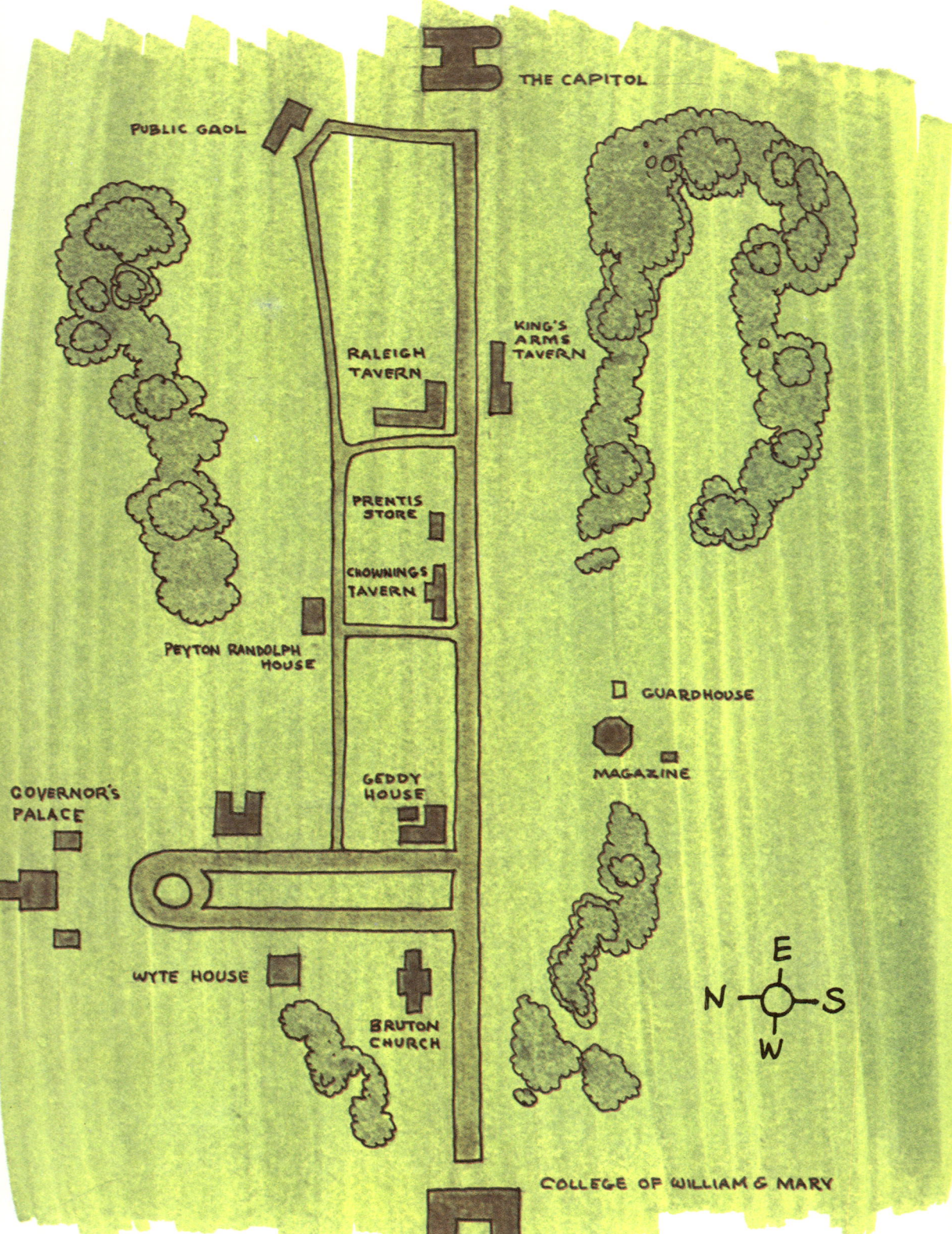

Chapter 2

BUILDING WILLIAMSBURG

In 1699 Williamsburg had a college, a church, several stores, a few houses, and an inn or two. People used only one street—an old horse path that ran from one end of town to the other.

The governor and burgesses were happy that Williamsburg was not built up. Because the town had so few buildings, they could build the city just the way they wanted it.

Nearly 300 acres of land was set aside for the new capital. The city was laid out in the shape of a rectangle. Plans called for a street 99 feet wide to run from one end of the capital to the other. The old horse path became this main street. Named for the Duke of Gloucester, it ran from west to east, beginning at the college.

Planners decided to place the Capitol building at the eastern end of Duke of Gloucester Street. The Capitol was planned in the shape of the letter H. On one side of the H the House of Burgesses met. The other side was used by the governor and his council. They had meetings and held the General Court. In 1704 the House of Burgesses and General Court began meeting in the new building.

Across from the Capitol was the public prison. It too was finished in 1704. At one time, 15 of Blackbeard's pirates were kept in this prison. After their trial, the pirates were hanged. Outside was a pillory where minor lawbreakers were publicly punished.

A committee of leading citizens made rules about how the city should look. Any house built in Williamsburg had to be on a half-acre lot. This space would leave plenty of room for a garden. Every house had to be at least six feet from the street. Each lot had to be fenced or walled in. The committee wanted the houses to look very much alike.

The houses in Williamsburg were built of brick or wood. They were built in the Georgian style, which was very popular in the eighteenth century. A Georgian house had its door in the middle. The same number of windows had to be on either side of the door. Windows on the second floor had to be placed directly above the ones on the first floor. If the house had a wing on one side, it was supposed to have a matching wing on the other side.

Behind each house was room for a garden of fruits, vegetables, and flowers. The kitchen was separate from the main house. Cooking meals in an outbuilding kept fires from getting started in the house. Besides cooking, the kitchen was also used for making candles, churning butter, and weaving cloth. Each lot might also have a smokehouse for curing meats and a stable for keeping livestock.

The roads along which these new houses were built had no paving or street lights. Often, carriages got stuck in muddy ruts. People always got dusty when there was no rain. At night, the streets were very dark. Folks had to put candles in their windows and hang lanterns by their doors to help travelers find their way.

Williamsburg's water highways were important means of transportation. Two ports were built, one on Queen's Creek, a second on Archer's Hope Creek. Each creek flowed into a river that ran into Chesapeake Bay or the

Atlantic Ocean. The creeks were deep enough for big trading ships to sail right up to the ports. Wharves for docking boats lined each port. Warehouses were also built to store tobacco and other crops.

In 1710 a new governor named Spotswood came to Virginia. He became very interested in making Williamsburg beautiful. First, Governor Spotswood planned a new church and gave a large sum of his own money for its building. In 1715, a rebuilt Bruton Parish Church was completed.

In that same year, Governor Spotswood planned a brick building for the storage of guns and powder. The building had five sides and a pointed roof. People called it the Powder Horn. Surrounded by a brick wall, the Powder Horn was set in a small green on Market Square.

Across Gloucester Street a Court House was built on the north side of Market Square. Here, the local government business of James County was carried out. Nearby stood Chowning's

Tavern, where out-of-town visitors could get a hot meal or play a game of cards.

Governor Spotswood's grandest undertaking was the Governor's House. Spotswood's plans cost a lot of money. The building and grounds were so beautiful that the people called it the Governor's Palace.

The palace was a brick mansion set among beautiful gardens. In front, it faced a large, open Green. In back of the house were neat walks, clipped hedges, gardens, and a fish pond.

Around the building was a brick wall. The entrance gate was made of wrought iron.

The palace was finished in 1720. Governor Spotswood gave a great dinner to show off the new house. At the mansion guests saw the most beautiful rooms in all Williamsburg. The mantlepieces were made of marble, the chandeliers of crystal. The doorways were framed in hand-carved wood. Dinner was served on silver dishes.

In 1722 Governor Spotswood retired to his plantation at Yorktown. He had worked hard to make the capital beautiful as well as useful. Under his direction, men had built some of the finest buildings in the New World.

In just 23 years Williamsburg had become the most important city in Virginia. It was the seat of colonial government. It was the educational hub for southern gentlemen going to college. And it was the social center for church meetings, market days, or holiday celebrations. Citizens living in Williamsburg enjoyed one of the most charming cities in the colonies.

Chapter 3
WILLIAMSBURG BECOMES IMPORTANT

During the eighteenth century, Virginia grew and prospered. No longer was the colony just a tiny settlement at Jamestown. New colonists arrived every year. There was more trade. Plantation-owners grew tobacco, wheat, corn, and flax. They sold these products to London merchants. Virginia was the richest of England's New World colonies.

Virginians agreed that William and Mary was one of the finest colleges in the colonies. Young men like Thomas Jefferson went there to study. Most of the teachers were ministers who had been educated in England. They taught such subjects as mathematics, Latin, physics, philosophy, and logic.

About 100 pupils enrolled in classes every year. Like students everywhere, they fussed about the bad food and cold classrooms. And, like all young men away from home for the first time, they got into trouble once in a while. Most of the time, however, they just played harmless tricks on one another. With all the fun, college was hard work.

Women did not attend the College of William and Mary. If women wanted an education they were tutored on a plantation or attended dame schools. Women were taught how to be ladies. Their education included sewing, drawing, dancing, and playing a musical instrument.

Williamsburg was a good place for young men interested in government and politics. For example, after Thomas Jefferson graduated from William and Mary, he studied law with a leading Williamburg lawyer. Being at the capital gave Jefferson the chance to attend meetings of the General Court. There, he learned how cases were argued in court.

Jefferson became a well-known lawyer. People trusted his judgment. They wanted Jefferson to run for office. He was only twenty-five years old when he won his first election. The voters of his county elected him to the House of Burgesses.

In 1736 William Parks began publishing a newspaper called the *Virginia Gazette.* Parks printed the first book of all Virginia's laws. He also opened a bookstore, where colonists could buy books, music, and stationery.

The *Virginia Gazette* kept people informed about news in other colonies. A postal service ran from New England to North Carolina. Mail was carried by post riders over rough, muddy roads. In 1753, English officials made William Hunter of Williamsburg and Benjamin Franklin of Philadelphia Postmasters.

Virginians usually visited Williamsburg during Publick Times. Publick Times took place twice a year, during spring and fall. At those times the House of Burgesses and General Court held their meetings.

Publick Times was a popular social time. During a Publick Time, the population of the city reached 3,000 or 4,000. Every room in every inn was filled. Sometimes people had to sleep six to a room. People who lived in Williamsburg all year opened their homes to guests and

relatives. Everyone enjoyed visiting and catching up on the news.

   The people of Williamsburg liked to copy English social life. They were not as strict about life as their northern neighbors, the Quakers and Puritans. Shops showed the latest clothes from London. At the governor's fancy dress balls, women wore rich brocades over hooped petticoats. The men dressed in satin knee breeches, velvet waistcoats, lace cuffs, and powdered wigs.

No one lacked for things to do during Publick Times. People enjoyed the Playhouse, where Shakespeare was performed by a London theater company. On Market Square, cakes, candies, cookies, and other treats could be bought at the stalls. There was plenty of fun—puppet shows, acrobats, cock-fighting, wrestling matches, and foot races.

Many joined a contest or two. As fiddlers played on the Green, people of all ages tried to win a pair of dancing pumps as a prize for their dancing. In one game, there was "A pig, with its tail soaped, to be run after; and to be given to

the person that catches him, and lifts him off the ground fairly by the tail."

The most popular spot in town was Raleigh Tavern, named for Sir Walter Raleigh. At the Raleigh, men talked politics over a mug of ale or played cards in the taproom. Cooks fixed fried chicken, sweet potatoes, corn bread, apple tarts, peach pie. There was country dancing in the evening. Outside, men played horseshoes or bowled on the green behind the tavern.

At Publick Times and during holidays, Williamsburg was crowded with people. Most of the year, however, the population numbered about 2,000 people. Unlike Boston or Philadelphia, Williamsburg never became a large seaport.

Virginia's network of river highways cut down on the growth of cities. The rivers let ships sail from one plantation to another. As a result, planters bought and sold goods directly with London merchants. What wasn't grown or made on the plantation could be bought by a planter right outside his own door. A family didn't need to use a town as a trading center. For this reason, Williamsburg stayed fairly small.

There were plenty of jobs in this busy capital. A workman had to be very skilled. Almost all work was done by hand.

A blacksmith made everything from horseshoes to wagon wheels and door locks. At the jewelry shop, the silversmith made shoe buckles, spoons, knives, and dishes of pewter and silver. The cobbler sewed shoes and boots to order, as well as tobacco boxes and leather

mugs. Other workers made furniture, cloth, soap and candles, guns, watches, carriages, hats, cabinets, and books.

Law-makers needed services while they stayed in the capital. Inns and rooming houses did a good business. Christiana Campbell's Tavern was George Washington's favorite spot when he came to town. The owner of a livery stable was busy, too. He rented horses and carriages. The town barber was a jack-of-all trades. He was skilled at giving his customers a shave, dressing a wig—even pulling teeth!

One of the busiest places in Williamsburg was Market Square. Every Wednesday and Saturday, farmers brought their crops to market. On those days, the square was crowded with people shopping at the stalls. There were chickens and pigs for sale, eggs and butter, fruits and vegetables of all kinds.

Market Square was in the center of Williamsburg. With the print shop and post office nearby, Market Square became the place to trade news.

During the spring of 1753, rumors flew through Market Square. Everyone was talking about the latest news in the *Virginia Gazette*. Articles reported that French troops from Canada had landed on the southern shore of Lake Erie. There, French soldiers had built forts. Indian spies friendly to the English colonists had also seen French troops building roads southward. They were cutting through the wilderness towards the Ohio Valley.

The people in Williamsburg were alarmed at this news. They wanted the rich lands west of Virginia for themselves. What right did the French have to these lands?

Then, more bad news reached the capital. The French had taken some English colonists prisoner for trading with the Indians. The French said the English were on their land. They said the lands of the Ohio Valley belonged to France.

The governor of Virginia acted quickly. He sent twenty-one-year-old George Washington, to warn the French away. The trip took Major Washington over two months in rough winter weather. When he got to the French fort, Washington delivered the governor's warning. At the same time, he was able to learn about French troops and French plans.

Washington rode back to Williamsburg with word from the French general. On February 14, 1754, the governor reported to the House of Burgesses. The French had no thought of returning to Canada. Over 1,500 French soldiers, along with their Indian allies, were getting ready to take over the whole Ohio Valley. By summer, the French would have new forts all along the Ohio River.

Chapter 4

PATRICK HENRY LEADS THE WAY

It was up to the Virginians. Either the French would take the rich western lands without a fight, or the English colonists would have to try and drive the French out of the valley.

Finally, after much talking, the House of Burgesses voted 10,000 pounds to be used to protect the frontier. The money was for soldiers and supplies. If the French wanted a fight, the Virginians would give them one!

A small group of men went to build a fort at the fork of the Ohio River. Then, in April of 1754, George Washington began marching westward to join them. With him were 160 men. Their job was to protect the new fort.

Before Washington and his men reached the Ohio River, a rider came dashing into camp. A force of 1,000 Frenchmen had attacked the Virginians' fort. The French now controlled the fork of the Ohio River. With so many Frenchmen at the oupost, Washington decided not to try and retake the fort.

Matters soon got worse. Washington and his men built a new outpost named Fort Necessity. There, they were attacked by a large force of French and Indians. The colonial forces were so outnumbered that Washington surrendered. He and his men were allowed to return to Virginia with the news of French victories.

The war was on! A lot was at stake. If the French won they would own the land from Canada to New Orleans. If the English won, then people from the 13 seaboard colonies could move westward. Both sides wanted the land, fur, fish, lumber, and game in the Ohio Valley.

By 1755 troops from England arrived to help the colonists fight the French and Indians. It was

an uphill battle for the English. They did not know the land as well as the French did. Also, the English could not get their 13 colonies to work with them. The French had much better helpers in their Indian allies. The one thing in England's favor was a good navy.

The fighting went on for several years. The war was like a see-saw. First the English would win a battle. Then the French would win a battle. Neither side could win enough battles to win the war.

Then, in 1759, General James Wolfe sailed up the St. Lawrence River to Quebec. Under his command was a large English force. The soldiers landed at night, climbed up a cliff near Quebec, and prepared for battle. The surprise worked. Although the French had more troops, they were defeated. This battle turned the tide in England's favor.

France and England signed a peace treaty in 1763. This treaty gave Canada to England. France also gave up all rights to the land between the Appalachian Mountains and the Mississippi River, including the Ohio Valley. The treaty left England with more than twice as much land in the New World as she had owned before the French and Indian War.

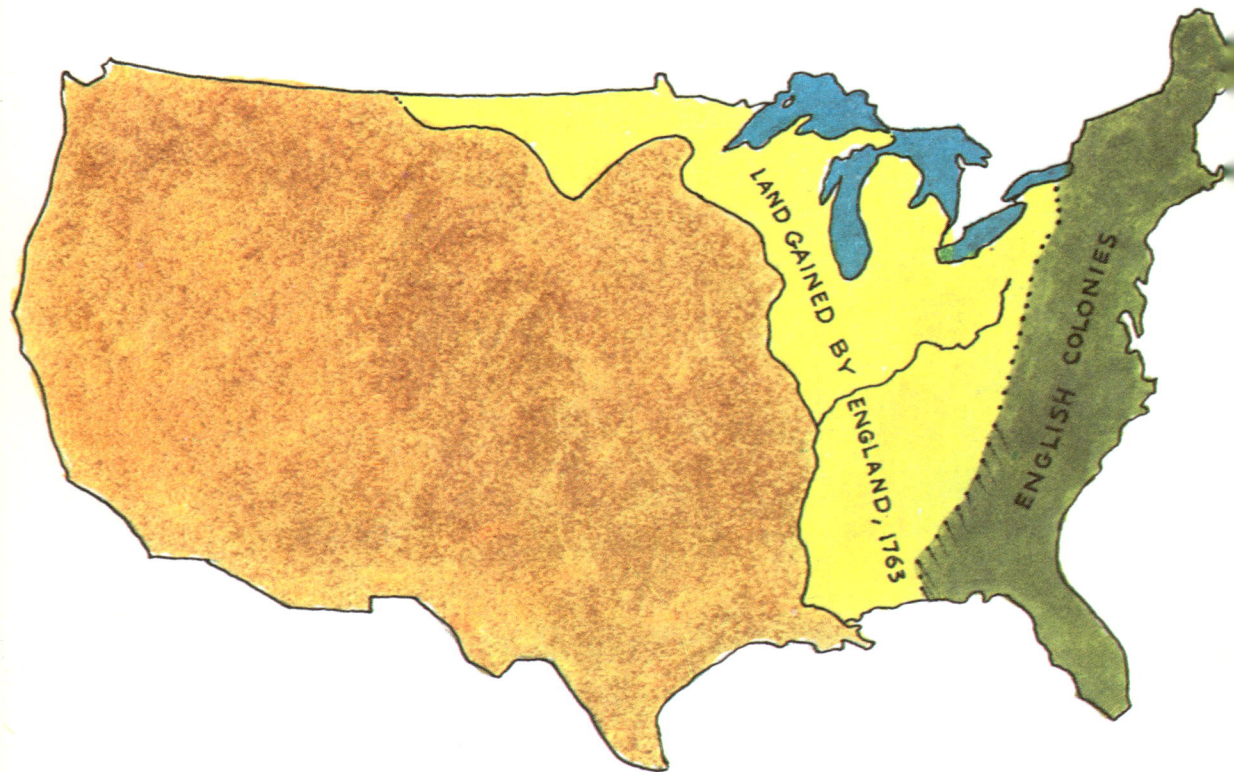

At first, the people of Virginia were happy about the English victory. Williamsburg was filled with stories about the new western lands. Already, settlers had crossed the Appalachian Mountains and started settlements at Pittsburg on the Ohio River and Boonesboro in Kentucky. In spite of Indian attacks, settlements kept on growing.

The English should have been happy about their victory, too. Instead, they began to worry. The war had cost England a lot of money. Moreover, it was going to cost even more money to protect all this new land England had won.

It was up to England's law-making body, called Parliament, to raise money. The cost of keeping English troops in North America would be high. Parliament did not want to raise taxes on the people living in England. Their taxes were already high. So, for the first time, Parliament decided to tax the colonies.

Parliament saw nothing wrong with this idea. Why shouldn't the colonists help pay part of defense costs? After all, said many members of Parliament, the colonists had the most to gain from a safe frontier.

In March of 1765, Parliament passed a law called the Stamp Act. The purpose of the Stamp Act was to raise money in the colonies. Every time a colonist bought a newspaper, pamphlet, or almanac, he had to pay a stamp tax. Stamps were also needed for wills, deeds, licenses, contracts—even playing cards.

When the colonial legislatures first heard about the tax law, they did not protest. From New Hampshire to Pennsylvania to Georgia, colonists seemed willing to pay the tax. Many colonists did not like the idea of a tax. Still, they thought it was their duty to obey the laws of Parliament.

In Williamsburg the House of Burgesses opened its spring meeting on May 1, 1765. It looked as if the Virginia legislature was going to go along with the Stamp Act like the other colonies. Then a new member of the burgesses took his seat. His name was Patrick Henry.

Patrick Henry was a backwoods lawyer from western Virginia. Some burgesses looked down on the newcomer because he didn't have much education. Others laughed at Henry's simple farm clothes.

All the same, the young lawyer was known throughout Virginia for his power to change men's minds. When Patrick Henry spoke, people listened.

Patrick Henry said just what was on his mind. On May 29, 1765, he rose in the House of Burgesses and began to speak against the Stamp Act. In his view, the Stamp Act took away the rights of the colonies. As long as the colonies didn't have any representatives in the English Parliament, then Parliament had no right to tax the colonists.

Henry's words made everyone think about their rights. In ringing tones, Henry said that only the House of Burgesses had the right to tax the Virginia colonists. He asked the members to support his statement.

When it came to a vote, the House of Burgesses agreed with Henry. They were against the right of Parliament to tax them.

News about the House of Burgesses' action traveled quickly. Newspapers as far north as New England printed the vote of the Virginia legislature. When other colonial legislatures met in the fall, they followed Williamsburg's lead. Many passed statements against the Stamp Act that were just like Patrick Henry's.

The colonists did more than just talk. In Boston, mobs gathered in the streets to protest the tax. They shouted "Liberty, Property, and no Stamps!" In many cities, colonists stopped buying English goods. They wanted to back up their words with action.

The outcry reached all the way across the Atlantic Ocean. London businessmen fussed because the Stamp Act was hurting their trade. Some members of Parliament agreed with Patrick Henry that taxation without representation was unfair. At last, on March 18,

1766, King George III signed a repeal of the Stamp Act. The tax was stopped.

When this news reached Virginia, the colonists were overjoyed. In Williamsburg, the governor declared a celebration. There were fancy dress balls, dinner parties, and firework displays. All over the capital, people raised their glasses to toast King George. Everyone felt loyal to England once again.

Chapter 5

"LIBERTY OR DEATH"

Repeal of the Stamp Act in 1766 did not settle the tax problem. England still needed money. As for King George, he still believed in Parliament's right to tax the colonies.

The colonists did not agree. They were willing to be taxed only by their own representatives. Besides, the colonists saw no need for English troops in their towns. Now that the French and Indian War was over, the colonists felt safe.

In spite of colonial feelings, Parliament passed another tax law in 1767. The law put a tax on lead, paint, glass, paper, and tea. The tax money would be used for defending the colonies.

King George was sure that his subjects would pay the taxes. He let it be known that he would not back down. This time, the law must be obeyed.

Word of the new tax law reached the colonies by autumn. In Williamsburg, the *Virginia Gazette* reported on Parliament's action.

The House of Burgesses felt the same way about these taxes as they did about the Stamp Act. They said that only the Virginia legislature had the right to tax Virginia colonists. Parliament could not tax them because no colonial representatives belonged to Parliament.

The House of Burgesses voted on their statements. They wanted the other 12 colonies to know where Virginia stood. They also sent a letter of their statements to King George. They asked him to read their statements carefully.

The burgesses backed up their words with deeds. They decided not to import English goods. The Virginians went along with this idea. They hoped this would hurt business in London. Then

English merchants would try and stop these taxes.

During the summer, most of the colonies followed Virginia's example. Colonial merchants in big cities would not import English products. Colonists either made their own goods or did without.

By 1770 the English were ready to give in. Parliament stopped most of the taxes. Only a tax on tea remained. Said King George, "There must always be one tax to keep up the right."

For the next few years, the people of Williamsburg went quietly about their business. Many did not drink tea, but they bought and used other English goods. The protests died down. It looked as if the problem was over.

Then, in 1773, trouble started once again. The people of Williamsburg learned that Boston colonists had protested against tea. Some men, dressed as Indians, had gone aboard English ships. Then they had thrown all the tea overboard into Boston Harbor.

England was not going to take this protest sitting down. For punishment, Parliament ordered the port of Boston closed. After June 1, 1774, no ships could go in or out of the harbor. The people of Boston would have to pay for the lost tea before the port could be opened again.

The colonists acted quickly. They held a meeting of all 13 colonies in Philadelphia. The meeting was called a Continental Congress. Each colony sent representatives. Williamsburg sent seven men to represent Virginia.

The Congress met in Philadelphia for several months. A Virginia representative was voted president of the Congress and Patrick Henry made the first speech. The representatives still hoped to work out their problems with England. But the Congress agreed that no colonies should import English goods. The Congress also told the colonists to arm themselves and form local militias for defense.

Virginia's representatives at the Congress returned to Williamsburg in November. The governor sided with the king and would not let the House of Burgesses meet. So the Virginians decided to meet on their own.

The governor heard what the colonists were going to do. When an English warship sailed near the city, the Virginia leaders knew it was not safe to meet in Williamsburg. The meeting place was moved westward, to Richmond. There the meeting began in March of 1775.

At the meeting in Richmond, Patrick Henry wanted Virginia to raise and arm a militia. Not everyone went along with his idea. Other members wanted Virginia to move slowly.

Patrick Henry rose to defend his idea. He said there was no longer any room for hope. The only thing left for the colonies to do was fight. When he spoke, the room became silent.

As he finished the speech, Patrick Henry's face grew pale, his eyes glared, and his voice rose louder and louder: "Is life so dear, or peace so sweet, as to be purchased at the price of chains and slavery?" he cried. "Forbid it, Almighty God!

I know not what course others may take, but as for me, give me liberty or give me death!"

Patrick Henry's idea was voted on and passed. Throughout Virginia, men began to form militias. They armed themselves with rifles and tomahawks. The hunting shirt became Virginia's military uniform. When the men heard about Patrick Henry's speech, some of the militiamen had "Liberty or Death" printed on their shirts. It looked as if war was not far off.

Chapter 6

VIRGINIA DECLARES INDEPENDENCE

The governor was frightened when he heard about the soldiers. He knew he needed help. On April 20, 1775, he sent a messenger to the nearby English warship. He ordered some English sailors to go to the Powder Horn. There, they were to remove the gunpowder.

In Williamsburg, the sailors were seen taking the gunpowder out of the city. Soon, drums sounded throughout the capital. The militia met and marched on the Governor's Palace. They demanded the return of the powder.

The people of Williamsburg were not the only ones in revolt. At the same time, fighting began in Massachusetts. On April 19, English troops and Massachusetts Minutemen fired on each other at Lexington and Concord. The shooting war had begun. "The sword is now drawn," said the *Virginia Gazette.*

Shortly after this fighting, the Congress of 13 colonies met again in Philadelphia. The representatives told the colonies to prepare for war. In June, the Congress voted George Washington the head of the American army.

In Virginia, the people began the war against England by getting rid of their hated governor. In May, Patrick Henry marched into Williamsburg with 150 followers. They demanded that the governor return the gunpowder he had taken from the city.

The frightened governor waited for a chance to run away. One night he was able to escape safely to the nearby English warship. With him went many people who were loyal to King George.

The governor was not ready to give up. On New Year's Day of 1776, he ordered the

English navy to set fire to the seaport of Norfolk. People could hardly believe such a beautiful city had gone up in flames.

This attack made the Virginians hopping mad. Loyalty to England melted like ice on a hot summer's day. More and more people began to talk about breaking away from England.

By spring, representatives in Williamsburg were ready to take the final step. The debate on independence began. A representative from Cumberland County spoke against further loyalty to King George. He said Virginia should "bid him Good Night forever."

Most of the representatives agreed. On May 15, 1776, the representatives voted in favor of Virginia's independence from England.

This declaration of independence was met with great joy in Williamsburg. The English flag was immediately taken down from the Capitol building. An American flag was raised in its place. The Virginia militia met on the Green, guns were fired, and soldiers paraded down Duke of Gloucester Street.

The Virginians did not wait to see what the other colonies thought of their move. They wanted to turn Virginia from a colony into a state. Williamsburg would be the capital.

By the end of June, the House of Burgesses met for the last time and then broke up. Virginians began to plan a new state government. This written plan of government was called a constitution. The Virginia Constitution was the first one in the colonies.

Meanwhile, the Virginia representatives had sent an express rider to the Continental

Congress meeting in Philadelphia. He told them what Virginia had done. He told the Virginia group that Virginia wanted all 13 colonies to declare independence together.

On June 7, Richard Henry Lee stood before the members of Congress. He said that the colonies should no longer be a part of England. He stated that the colonies "are, and of right ought to be, free and independent states."

The Congress decided not to vote on this idea right away. The representatives wanted time to find out what people back home wanted. At the same time, the Congress picked a committee to write a Declaration of Independence.

For the next three weeks, Thomas Jefferson wrote and re-wrote a Declaration of Independence. Benjamin Franklin and John Adams were on the committee with him, but they thought Jefferson could do the best job. Franklin and Adams made only small changes in Jefferson's final copy.

On July 2, 1776, the Congress voted on Richard Henry Lee's statement of independence. All but one colony voted to break away from England. Two days later, Congress voted for Jefferson's Declaration of Independence. John Hancock signed it. Later most members of the Congress also signed it.

The Declaration of Independence was printed in many newspapers. It was read to cheering crowds throughout the new states.

The Declaration of Independence gave people a feeling of faith in themselves. It said every person had certain rights that no one else could take away. The Declaration showed a basic respect for human beings.

The idea that all men are free and equal was a new one to many people. Some thought ideas about freedom and equality were dangerous. Certainly, most plantation-owners did not think the Declaration meant they should free their slaves.

Still, the Declaration of Independence was important. It took a stand for human rights. Freedom and equality became goals for the new United States.

Chapter 7

A FORGOTTEN CITY

The new government of Virginia elected Patrick Henry their first governor. He remained governor for three years, until 1779.

Henry and his government had many problems to solve. The English controlled the sea. They fired on Virginia's seaport cities.

On the western frontier, the English had made friends with the Indians. The wilderness settlements were in great danger. Indians began attacking American forts. Virginia had to send soldiers to fight the Indians. This made the English happy, because it took soldiers away from the American army.

The best frontier fighter was a man named George Rogers Clark. He came before the lawmakers in Williamsburg to report what was happening in the west. Governor Henry asked support for Clark. The legislature gave Clark guns and powder.

During the next two years, Clark won many battles. His men captured three English forts and the hated English governor of Detroit. This governor was known for paying Indians to scalp the Americans. Clark's prisoners were booed when they arrived in the capital.

After three years in office, Governor Henry retired. On June 1, 1779, 36-year-old Thomas Jefferson was elected governor.

Soon after his election, Governor Jefferson tried to get the capital moved. Many people had settled in Virginia since Williamsburg had become the capital in 1699. It was no longer in a central position. Besides, Jefferson argued, Williamsburg was not safe from attacks by the English navy.

Governor Jefferson wanted the capital moved to Richmond. It was further west than Williamsburg. Its location was easier for more people to reach. Richmond was safer because it was further from the coast.

The law-makers argued and debated. Many agreed that Richmond was in a more central place, but they enjoyed Williamsburg. They liked its broad streets and beautiful buildings.

On June 12, they decided to move to Richmond. By the spring of 1780, Williamsburg was no longer the capital.

Just the same, exciting times were not yet over for Williamsburg. The war was still on, and in 1781 it came to Virginia. Nearly 8,000 English troops under General Cornwallis attacked the state. The government was not even safe in Richmond, and Governor Jefferson was almost captured.

Toward the end of June, Cornwallis brought his troops into Williamsburg. The soldiers camped on the Green and on the college grounds. They broke into houses and took what they wanted. They ate at the inns without paying. There was nothing anyone could do.

After ten days, Cornwallis moved his troops to Yorktown. The people were afraid he would set Williamsburg on fire when he left. Instead, he burned all the crops at nearby plantations. He took livestock with him to feed his men.

No sooner had Cornwallis left than General Washington arrived. With him were about 16,000 American and French troops. Once again, the streets were filled with soldiers. Only this time the men were friendly.

In Williamsburg, Washington and his generals drew up a plan. They figured out a way to surround the English at Yorktown.

By September, Washington was ready to put his plan into action. As he left Williamsburg, the people cheered him on his way. They hoped the war would soon be over.

The trap at Yorktown worked, but it took many weeks. During that time, wounded soldiers were brought into Williamsburg. The Governor's Palace was turned into a hospital. The palace gardens became a graveyard for American soldiers.

On October 19, 1781, General Cornwallis surrendered at Yorktown. This was the last important battle of the Revolution. The United States of America had won independence.

The people of Williamsburg were overjoyed when they heard about Yorktown. They were proud of Washington because he was a Virginian. He was everyone's hero.

When American and French soldiers returned to Williamsburg, they received a joyful welcome. Flags flew from every window. Cannon sounded from the Green. Happy crowds cheered the soldiers on parade, and parties went on for days.

After the war was over, few people visited the former capital to trade or do business. The best workmen and businessmen moved to Richmond.

The buildings in Williamsburg were not kept in good repair. The Governor's Palace burned down. Goats and cattle roamed the streets. The gardens and parks were overgrown with weeds.

As time passed, Williamsburg became a forgotten city. Few people remembered its part in the move for independence. Williamsburg's best days were gone forever.

Williamsburg remained a forgotten city for 145 years. Then, in 1926, John D. Rockefeller became interested in the old town. He wanted to rebuild Williamsburg so people could see how it had looked in the eighteenth century.

It took many years to rebuild Williamsburg. Architects studied old plans to see how the city had been laid out. Some old buildings still remained standing. But others had to be rebuilt. Every effort was made to re-create the city.

Today, a visit to Williamsburg is like going back 200 years in time. William and Mary, where Jefferson went to college, is still there. So too is the Powder Horn, where English sailors removed gunpowder in 1775. And visitors can see the Capitol building where Patrick Henry spoke against the Stamp Act, and Virginians declared their independence from England.

Williamsburg's inns still serve the public. Christiana Campbell's Tavern, a favorite of Washington, serves food in the southern tradition. Waiters wear the same clothes people wore at the time of the Revolution.

Campbell's Tavern

Colonial Williamsburg Photograph

Duke of Gloucester Street

As visitors walk the streets of Williamsburg, they can see the same shops the colonists used. A variety of colonial goods is on display. Workmen can be seen making candles and soap, boots and shoes, pewter and silver by hand. Cloth is woven on wooden looms. Bread is baked in fiery brick ovens. Even furniture is made by hand, using old-fashioned tools.

If you ever visit Williamsburg, don't expect to see any cars. Transportation is by horse and carriage. Or, you could do as most colonists did—walk!

Gunsmith

Bootmaker

About the Authors:

Susan Dye Lee has been writing professionally since she graduated from college in 1961. Working with the Social Studies Curriculum Center at Northwestern University, she has created course materials in American studies. Ms. Lee has also co-authored a text on Latin America and Canada, written case studies in legal history for the Law in American Society Project, and developed a teacher's guide for tapes that explore women's role in America's past. The writer credits her students for many of her ideas. Currently, she is doing research for her history dissertation on the Women's Christian Temperance Union for Northwestern University. In her free moments, Susan Lee enjoys traveling, playing the piano, and welcoming friends to "Highland Cove," the summer cottage she and her husband, John, share.

John R. Lee enjoys a prolific career as a writer, teacher, and outdoorsman. After receiving his doctorate in social studies at Stanford, Dr. Lee came to Northwestern University's School of Education, where he advises student teachers and directs graduates in training. A versatile writer, Dr. Lee has co-authored the Scott-Foresman social studies textbooks for primary-age children. In addition, he has worked on the production of 50 films and over 100 filmstrips. His biographical film on Helen Keller received a 1970 Venice Film Festival award. His college text, *Teaching Social Studies in the Elementary School*, has recently been published. Besides pro-football, Dr. Lee's passion is his Wisconsin cottage, where he likes to shingle leaky roofs, split wood, and go sailing.

About the Artist:

Tom Dunnington divides his time between book illustration and wildlife painting. He has done many books for Childrens Press, as well as working on textbooks, and is a regular contributor to "Highlights for Children." He is at present working on his "Endangered Wildlife" series, which is being reproduced as limited edition prints. Tom lives in Elmhurst.